365
SEX TIPS

DUMONT
monte

Copy editing: A.P.E. Overath
Cover design: BOROS, Wuppertal

© 2000 DuMont Buchverlag, Cologne
(Dumont monte UK/London)

© cover illustration:
folio ID/Obert-Huber (left&right)
Tony Stone (middle)

ISBN 3-7701-7007-5
Printed in Slovenia

The right atmosphere is essential for achieving real sexual pleasure. Quiet music helps induce a relaxed atomosphere beforehand, while more intense music can increase desire and help to reduce inhibitions. Try to discover which music brings you the most pleasure.

2

Stash the remote control for the stereo next to the bed so you can change the musical mood without having to kill the moment.

3

BED

Don't get caught up in the idea of keeping up a perfectly-made bed—toss some throw pillows on the bedspread to create an inviting space for cuddling.

Keep Francis Bacon out of the bedroom! Aggressive or depressing pictures or posters in such an intimate space don't promote a sense of sensual relaxation.

4

5

Create a sensuous and loving space by filling your bedroom with photographs of your favourite holidays and romantic moments.

6

FLOWER POWER

Rose petals spread all over a bed not only look inviting, they also smell wonderful. Dive into a sea of sensuality.

7

Indoor plants create a rejuvenating, vibrant atmosphere. You can achieve all sorts of striking effects with romantic blossoms or wild vines. Surround yourself with your favourite flowers and plants.

A large mirror in which you and your partner can see yourselves while making love can enhance your senses and your fantasies.

9

Comfort is key! Hindrances like bookshelves surrounding the head of the bed are at the very least an impediment to freedom of movement, and at worst can be dangerous. Line your bed with pillows and ensure that the room is at a comfortable temperature.

10

Get rid of a squeaking bed as quickly as possible. It's a serious mood killer—for you and your next door neighbours. Until the new bed arrives, seek out an alternative: the sofa, the kitchen table, the grand piano.... make necessity a virtue and be inventive.

11

If you have children, make it a habit to get away for the weekend now and then, just the two of you. If you know the kids are in good hands, you can truly savour your free time: in a sauna, at the movies, with a romantic candlelight dinner, or even a day in bed.

12

Rid your immediate
surroundings—especially the
bedroom—of all the things that
inhibit intimacy. The telephone,
the computer, and the television
are antithetical to real connection.

13

Even the colour palette of your surroundings play an important role while making love. Test which colours are most engaging and which most relaxing for you and your partner—then get out the paint brushes...

14

Cover your bed with soft fabrics that caress the skin. Satin and suede feel soft and supple, and can either warm or cool the skin. Give some thought to your bedding as well, so that the colours and patterns complement the rest of the room.

15

Bright or harsh lighting (such as neon) can kill a sense of seduction. Traditional candlelight, which still creates the best mood, contributes to a sensual atmosphere. A dimmer can also create light with the right degree of illumination.

16

Scent is the crowning touch to every atmosphere, which is why scented candles, essential oils in an oil lamp or even incense are ideal accessories for lovemaking. The variety available these days is virtually endless, so experiment and find exactly the scent that suits you.

17

Keep condoms, dildos or vibrators handy and nearby to prevent irritating interruptions or risk spoiling a wonderful mood while you search for the perfect love toy.

18

Surprise your partner by receiving him in nothing but tantalizing lingerie. If you like it even hotter, slide into some high heels and place red lightbulbs in a few lamps.

19

Make sure you have ventilation in your bedroom so that you can breath freely and deeply. Fresh air is also a good antidote against sleepiness.

20

Arrange a rendezvous in a café with your partner and pretend that you are only just getting to know each other. This can turn into an exciting flirtation and help liberate you from constricting habits.

The pressures of daily life are antithetical to sexual desire. It's crucial to relax completely, switch off your professional self, and leave the hectic world outside before having sex.

Here is a relaxing mixture you might want to try in your oil lamp:

1 drop of rose oil,
2 drops of ylang-ylang oil, and
3 drops of sandlewood oil in a little water.

21

22

Choose a certain day of the month on which your or your partner's every wish will be fulfilled. Make these "X-Days" a permanent item on your (love-) calendar.

23

Take sufficient time for sex—and increase your pleasure by savouring a gradual increase in desire. Time pressure is a major stress factor that decreases your sexual energy.

24

To relax, take off your clothes and lie down comfortably on your back, close your eyes and focus on simply feeling your body.

25

Concentrate on areas where you still feel tense and stroke your body there, or better yet, ask your partner to do so. Feel the touch release the tension like a gentle massage.

26

Taking slow, deep breaths, in through the nose and out through the mouth, induces genuine relaxation. (Fast, shallow breathing counteracts relaxation!)

Try this breathing exercise together with the following: Rub your palms together firmly for at least a half minute and then hold them up to your partner's at a distance of about 4 inches. At first you'll notice warmth and a tingling sensation, and then a sense of energy will develop between your hands. You and your partner can then play with this energy by slowly moving your hands back and forth.

A simple bubble bath also does wonders for relaxation. However, do not stay in the bath so long that you get sleepy–it should be a sexual aid, not a soporific.

27

28

You may have already noticed at the hair salon—a head massage is particularly relaxing (not to mention arousing). Why not try it with your partner?

Massage the skin of your partner's head gently first, then with increasing pressure. In between, use all your fingers to stroke your partner's hair. Don't neglect to revive the temples and neck with gentle circles of your fingertips.

An ear massage also breaks the routine: Take your partner's ears and earlobes between two fingers of each hand and rub them gently. Then massage the edge of the ears with circling motions and finally, block out daily life completely by covering the ears with your flat hand and making gentle rotations.

29

30

A foot massage is, of course, a particularly good way to relax. A lukewarm footbath, topped off with 2 or 3 drops of jasmine oil, can be a wonderful starter.

To begin, alternate a light and a strong grasp of the whole foot from heel to toe, then stroke the foot from the centre out to the periphery several times, up- and downward. Finally, massage the toes individually. Don't forget to take turns!

31

A tense jaw muscle is a sure sign that you are holding back your emotions—not to mention your natural voice. You can easily relax your jaw by letting your lower jaw drop instead of pressing your teeth together. Automatically, the tongue, the larynx and the face relax, and you also become more open emotionally.

32

Especially in winter, hands easily become chapped and have a less pleasant effect when stroking someone you care for. Try making a mixture of equal parts glycerine, lemon juice, and honey. If you rub some of it into your hands every day, they will stay soft and supple. Let the mixture soak into your skin for a few minutes, then rinse off the rest.

33

Buttermilk can make a bath into an unforgettable (and even addictive) experience. Add 1 litre of buttermilk and 2 tablespoons of honey to warm bath water; sprinkle in a few rose petals, and turn off the bathroom lights.

34

Create a your own scented sachets. Combine 20g of fresh rosemary leaves, 20g of fresh peppermint leaves, 50g of dried rose petals, 5 crushed cloves, and 3 drops of patchouli oil on a piece of cotton wool, and slip a fabric cover over it. Place in a pillow or a drawer.

35

Celery is a known aphrodisiac, so why not try a Waldorf Salad? You will need 250g potatoes and 250g peeled celery, both steamed and diced. Add 250g peeled, cored, and chopped apples and 1 or 2 chopped pickles. Combine all the ingredients in a bowl and sprinkle with 1 tablespoon nuts. For the sauce, use a fork to beat 3 tablespoons salad oil, 1 to 2 tablespoons vinegar, and a pinch of salt with a fork. Add 1 teaspoon finely chopped herbs and mayonnaise to taste. Mix the sauce with the rest of the ingredients and let the salad stand briefly to let the flavours mingle.

36

Caviar is such a delicious, luxurious aphrodisiac that it is best served simply on lightly buttered toast.

37

Like the aphrodisiac lovage, which has a strongly stimulating effect, herbs can influence our physical well-being and our libido.

The succulent stems of the angelica plant revive and strengthen the nervous system, and have a pleasantly bitter-spicy flavour when used in cooking.

The sweet-spicy taste of chervil lends itself to a variety of uses in the kitchen. In addition to cleansing the blood, it helps reduce blood pressure, which has a calming and stress-combating effect.

Parsley is not only a pretty decoration, it also has a high vitamin content and stimulates respiration, as well as strengthening the immune system.

38

Why not make yourself literally "hot"? A large pinch of hot chilli in your food can raise your temperature and your partner's.

39

Oysters are probably the most famous epicurean aphrodisiac, in part because the eating itself is an erotic pleasure—both for the one who is eating and the one who is watching. Treat yourself and your partner to a sybaritic feast of love.

40

A glass of champagne can often work wonders. Combined with strawberries—which are also stimulating—you have a classic combination that you simply must try!

FORBIDDEN FRUIT

41

Fresh fruit also has aphrodisiacal properties, in particular strawberries, grapes, cherries and fresh figs. As always, the more sensuously you partake of the sweet little fruits, the greater their effect!

42

Stroke your partner from head to toe, first lying on their back and then on the stomach, and consciously leaving out the genitals to start with. Trade places and let yourself be stroked by your partner in the same way, then make a second round in which you include the genital area. You are sure to experience an intense build-up of desire.

Discover your personal erogenous zones.
Every person experiences touch of various
parts of the body differently. Do you
particularly enjoy being stroked on the neck
or is it more tantalizing to be caressed up
and down your back?

44

WITH SKIN AND HAIR

Your hands are not the only way to touch your partner—let you
imagination run wild. Your tongue, hair, fingernails and nipples have
very special effects on your partner's skin.

43

45

Vary the sensations by using feathers, fabrics, a powder puff or a soft brush. Dip the brush in fragrant oil and then "paint" your partner with it for a many-splendored experience.

46

DESK JOBS

Most people nowadays work seated at a desk. Unfortunately, spending so much time sitting has a weakening effect on our libido. Those who do not make sports part of their regular routine can still increase the circulation of blood to their pelvic region by standing with their legs slightly apart and circling their hips in one direction and then the other.

47

Stimulate yourself before lovemaking by lying on your back with your knees bent. Raise your pelvis and lower back and hold that position. After a while, lower them again and enjoy the warm feeling in your groin.

48

Relax your Genital Area:

Women crouch with their arms inside of their knees and place the palms of their hands flat on the floor.

Men take one of their testicles in each hand, pull gently downward and then release them (repeat several times).

49

Massage your partner's erogenous zones with a scented massage oil (warm the massage oil and your hands first!). To finish off the massage, run your fingernails over the area. That tingles!

50

Breathing is not only important for relaxation. Your warm breath on your partner's various erogenous zones has a reassuringly tender and deliciously stimulating effect.

With stimulating touch, just as in love-making itself, variety is the A and O. Your touch should never be predictable for your partner, so vary your technique (circling with the whole palm of your hand, only with the fingertips, running your palms or fingertips up and down, etc.) as well as the speed and the pressure you exert.

51

52

Give your voice the freedom it needs and don't try to suppress your moans or cries. This freedom will enable you—but also your partner—to experience more intense sexual feeling.

53

If you have difficulty letting go of sensual sounds, try it by yourself to start with.

Make sure you will be alone at home for a while and prepare yourself with a relaxing bath and pleasant music. Devote yourself entirely to your body—start with slow stroking of your erogenous zones, concentrating on your breathing, and listen to your vocal response.

54

HAIRY

Hair is one of the oldest aids to stimulation. Drag your hair over your partner's body. If you have long hair, leaning over your partner and lightly swinging it over your partner's skin can be very erotic.

55

Spoil your partner's erogenous zones with your lips and tongue. Make sure you vary your technique, speed, and pressure to arouse the maximum desire in your partner..

56

Whole body contact is not only stimulating, but also conveys a profound feeling of security, increasing trust in both partners. While your partner lies on her or his stomach, glide slowly up and down pressing your genitals against the back and buttocks. When lying on your sides, face to face, you can increase the intensity through eye contact.

57

Gently stroke your partner's inner thighs—gently or somewhat more firmly—before gradually making your way towards the pubic area. This can increase desire to a fever pitch.

58

Circle the tip of the clitoris with a finger, then gently rub up and down on the shaft of the clitoris to stimulate your partner with increasing intensity.

For a different effect, try touching the vulva as lightly as possible.

59

To increase a man's desire and excitement, hold his erect penis in the centre with one hand while gently running your other hand over the tip and shaft of the penis.

Men can postpone their climax by exerting pressure on the Jen-Mo-spot, which lies between the scrotum and the anus, shortly before an orgasm. If sufficient pressure is exerted, this prevents the passage of semen through the urethra. It is best for men to locate the Jen-Mo-spot on their own at first. If you press too closely to the scrotum, the semen may flow into the bladder instead of the blood (as is intended), resulting in whitish urine after sex. If you press too closely to the anus, orgasm will not be prevented.

A man's orgasm can also be controlled by having one of the partners pull his scrotum downward.

To prolong a woman's pleasure, stop the action shortly before she reaches climax and then resume the stimulation with slower movements.

61

62

Mens' nipples are highly
sensitive and receptive to
stimulation of every kind: kissing,
stroking with the hand or lips or
tongue or...

63

Don't do anything solely to give your partner pleasure; only do what you really enjoy. This approach is the best way to ensure maximum pleasure for both partners.

64

Hector's Horse

In this position, the woman sits on the man with her knees at his sides. He can penetrate deeply as she sits up and leans her back against his knees, which are bent and drawn up toward his body.

65

Stagecoach

The partners sit opposite each other, she on his lap with her legs around his hips or on his shoulders, while he has his legs below her. Support yourselves with your hands behind you.

If she sits atop the man facing backward (the man lies on his back), she can stroke his scrotum during penetration. If she leans back onto him and supports her weight with her arms, he can stroke her clitoris during penetration.

Missionary Position

In what is probably the most famous position, the man lies on the woman, stomach to stomach, and carries his weight by supporting himself with his arms. The strength of this position is that it is possible to have both eye and kissing contact.

He can penetrate especially deeply if she lies on her back with one or both legs over his shoulders while he penetrates from the front.

67

Positions Next to Each Other

These positions require less physical exertion, and neither partner is constrained by the weight of the other. The resulting freedom of movement allows you to easily roll around the bed together. Face to face, partners should use the opportunity to whisper intimacies.

68

Positions From Behind

The positions from behind can be useful when trust between the partners has not developed to the point that they can show each other everything.

The lack of eye contact can make it easier for both partners to really let themselves go.

69

Two Fish
In this position, the partners lie on their sides, face to face. The woman can place her legs over his during penetration.

Flying Seagulls

She lies on her back with her buttocks on the edge of the bed, while he kneels in front of her and penetrates. In this position, the penis and vagina are parallel to one another, allowing a completely different type of stimulation than usual.

70

Frog Position

The man sits upright with his legs stretched out straight, while the woman lies in front of him with her knees drawn toward herself and held in her arms. Her head is raised to such an extent that he can hold her shoulders with his hands.

The freedom of motion in this position is very limited, but it conveys a strong sense of safety and closeness.

Outcry Position

While the woman sits face to face on top of the man, he sits so that her bent knees hang over his elbows. After penetration he holds on to her sides below her breasts and moves her back and forth.

72

73

During penetration, exerting gentle pressure on the lower part of a man's penis with a free hand will excite him further.

In positions from behind, a man can give a woman great pleasure if he rotates his hips while penetrating. This stimulates the vagina in many unusual places.

74

75

The navel is very sensitive and an ideal location for erotic games, since it is near the genital area. Fill your partner's navel with champagne and allow her or him to enjoy the prickling sensation for a while. Then use tongue and lips to try to reach the delicious liquid...

76

Hands are very sensitive to gentle touch. Try devoting yourself exclusively to your partner's hands, making sure to maintain eye contact while you do!

Step 1: Begin with a stroking massage of the back of the hands, then move on to the more sensitive palm, and don't forget the fingers.

Step 2: Repeat the entire process, but this time cover your partner's hands with kisses, trace the lines on the palm with your tongue, or nibble lightly on their fingertips. Let your imagination run wild.

77

SPLISH, SPLASH!

If you have a bathtub, you should definitely include it in your intimate life. Warm water relaxes the body, so make sure that the temperature remains pleasant. Candles can provide a romantic atmosphere in an otherwise rather sterile and overly bright bathroom. Adding an aphrodisiac bath salt or bubbles will release a wonderful aroma. Prepare a little snack and something to drink—you shouldn't have any trouble coming up with something for dessert!

Owing to the dangers of HIV infection and the prevalence of sexually transmitted diseases, it should be a matter of course to use a condom during sexual intercourse. Condoms now exist in every imaginable shape, colour and flavour.

Putting on a condom need not be an interruption, but can instead be integrated into foreplay.

If you have "hand sex," latex gloves or fingers protect both partners from HIV infection.

78

79

Learning to love yourself as you are is the root and foundation of your sexual desire. Look into a mirror while stroking yourself over your whole body, and concentrate on yourself fully. This sensual self-awareness frees you for the pleasures of a genuinely satisfying sexuality.

Avoid abrupt changes from one
type of touch to the next. Instead, take
your time, indulge and fully explore
the depth of each individual form of
contact.

81

The shower is an ideal spot for erotic games. The warm water is relaxing, and body contact under a stream of water is more intense. Soap each other up from head to toe—it's nice and slippery, and what happens next is up to you!

82

Articulate your wishes to your partner. Without genuine and open communication, your sex life can easily become routine.

Absolute trust in each other is vital for satisfying sex. You can build this trust by honest discussions and frequent massages.

83

Make a date with your partner for a day or a period of time in which you both go about your business at home—naked. You will find that your fantasy is unleashed. Suddenly your entire home is an erotic playground!

A MATTER OF TASTE

Sex games with food are extraordinarily "tasteful." Physical love should try to stimulate all of our senses—so don't neglect your sense of taste!

Let your partner spread whipped cream over several parts of your body and then lick it off again. Or let grapes roll over your partner's body and nibble on them wherever they land.

85

If your powers of imagination should be running low, try watching an erotic film together, one you have both agreed on in advance. The selection process alone can tell you a lot about your partner's erotic preferences.

86

A loofah glove increases the circulation in your skin. Rub your partner's body (not too firmly) with a glove or sponge. When the skin just begins to turn red, stroke it lightly with the tips of your fingers—that tingles!

87

Give your partner erotic accessories as a gift occasionally—ribbed condoms for him, a garter belt for her, perhaps a vibrator for both of you—to be used according to your desires!

Many women find the following breast massage highly stimulating: Use a finger to trace a spiral from the outside to the inside of one breast, and then the other. Softly squeeze the skin around the nipple between your index finger and thumb, then move your fingers over the skin in this manner toward the edge of the breast. To finish off, press the nipple gently between your index finger and thumb and glide upwards.

89

TANTALIZING TOUR

Lead your partner's hands on a "tour" of your own body. This will be a completely unexpected pleasure for both of you.

90

Prolonged foreplay is not only important for her, but also induces strong desire in him.

Most people find it highly arousing to receive gentle kisses on their ear lobes. The neck is another particularly erogenous zone. Spoil it with delicate strokes and kisses!

91

Arouse your partner with "love bites"—gently grip their skin with your teeth and move it back and forth. Naturally, not every area of skin is designed to accommodate nibbling, but some are particularly suited for it: The neck and the inside of the thighs are extremely sensitive to biting.

Tongue the skin while you gently bite with your teeth to create a fascinating combination of biting and kissing, hard and soft.

92

Caress your partner's body with your open mouth so that just your teeth touch the skin, scintillatingly threatening to bite unexpectedly at any moment.

93

Masturbating each other can be not only very stimulating, but also helps you learn each other's preferences and dislikes.

94

Try having sex somewhere other than in bed. Change is a crucial element in a fulfilled sex life. For example, sex out of doors should be tried not only for the fresh air—the possibility of getting caught creates a special sense of danger and excitement.

95

THE JOYS OF SUMMER

The sun is shining—suffering from spring fever? Surprise your partner during the lunch break with an unexpected visit and an invitation to join you for a frolic in a park.

96

Summer, sunshine, and picnics: When was the last time you and your partner enjoyed Mother Nature? Do it often—and fully! Search out a clearing in the woods, a lake, or an isolated beach, taking care that your destination doesn't require a long travel time. Begin with a romantic walk hand-in-hand, looking for a private spot for your picnic for two. You may find that your "meal" consists of something more than what you brought along in your basket...

97

Sex is not a competition, so there is no need to put yourself under pressure to reach a climax as quickly as possible. This psychological attitude can spoil the atmosphere and lead to frustration.

98

Platform shoes lengthen the legs and require a heightened sense of bodily self-consciousness. This makes them exciting for both partners, the wearer and the observer. Why not glide through life five inches taller for a while? Red patent leather shoes also send clear signals. There is another advantage—sex while standing can be more relaxed and less of an acrobatic feat!

99

A vibrator or a dildo can increase your mutual pleasure, beginning with the purchase itself. Have fun looking at different models, and allowing the anticipation to mount. At home you should slowly become accustomed to the new "toy." Find out where and how the vibrations are especially exciting for you. Express the child in you, and let your curiosity run wild!

Women often enjoy having their labia and clitoris gently stroked with the vibrator before inserting it, and some men like to have the vibrator inserted in their anus.

One more note—dildos and vibrators can be wonderful aids to masturbation, too...

100

Tell each other your erotic fantasies. This can be an arousing prelude to great sex. How about telling each other a story or making up a play in several "acts" and then taking turns performing individual scenes?

101

BLIND MAN'S BLUFF

Playing blind man's bluff develops trust between partners, and is a lot of fun at the same time. It is best to take turns. Both people should be naked, and one is blind-folded. Gently stroke your "blind" partner with brushes, fruits, cloth, etc., and let her or him guess what you are using, or surprise your partner by rubbing their body with oil, leading them into a shared warm bath, or whatever else occurs to you. Whatever you do, make sure that your movements and touch are not abrupt and that the temperature is comfortable. This is not a good time to try out new "toys," as any negative experiences would quickly ruin the relaxed and trusting atmosphere.

Women, take note—men also like to be seduced! Approach your partner and make the first move.

Why not perform a strip-tease? Undress slowly and seductively in front of your partner to excite her or him.

103

Whispering descriptions of erotic images during lovemaking can be incredibly seductive.

We also tend to associate exotic and erotic images with the sound of another language. So why not try a foreign language at the peak of your lovemaking? "Je t'aime" or "ti amo" can work like magic—and you don't have to go through customs to say them.

104

EROTIC TREASURE HUNT

One way to seduce your partner is to leave a trail of erotic underwear through the apartment—leading, of course, to you! Stockings lying in the hall, a bra hanging from the doorknob, you naked on the sofa—who could resist?

105

While making love, imagine you are the main characters in an erotic film—and give each other stage directions. Or take on the roles of characters in a movie you have watched together, perhaps Valérie Kaprisky and Richard Gere in *Breathless*.

106

A fantasy that some people find arousing is to imagine a large audience standing around you, cheering on you and your partner while you are having sex.

107

HOT KISSES

Try oral sex the other way around—your partner's mouth is the passive part that is kissed by the penis or vagina.

108

HOT SPOTS

Go through your home and identify every spot in which you can imagine having sex. Then make a list with your partner, and plan to try all of the listed spots, one after the other, within a set amount of time. Or write all the places on small pieces of paper and before the next time you have sex, one of you draws the next "scene of the crime" out of a hat.
Or stash one of those small pieces of paper in your partner's jacket pocket. Or send your partner an email at work with the rendevous location. Or…

109

Try to arrange a weekend getaway for two to a cozy little hotel in the country, and let yourselves be inspired by the romantic peacefulness of nature to fully and completely concentrate on your love play.

110

You can be 17 forever...

Go the movies together and relive your teenage dreams in the last row. The film—and we're not talking about *The Lion King*—will be even more exciting if neither of you is wearing underwear...

111

Meet your partner in a hotel and pretend you are having a clandestine affair. The affair is even more exciting if it is arranged spontaneously and you arrive separately.

Hot Secrets

Sometime while you are
on the phone with your
partner, drop a comment
out of the blue like "I'd like
to undress you right now,"
or "I'm imagining that I'm
nuzzling your earlobe."
You will immediately hear
the impact you have on
your unsuspecting partner!

112

113

COOL:

Run an ice cube slowly and smoothly over your partner's body until it has melted.

114

SUSPENSE:

Imagine you are making an anonymous call to the police while your partner is stimulating you, but don't let your voice give you away. Hold back as long as you can, releasing with a great moan when the tension is unbearable.

115

CALL ME!

Telephone sex can also be simulated. Go into another room where your partner can hear but not see you—and then tell each other your erotic fantasies.

116

MUSEUM PIECE

Imagine you are a sculpture in a museum and your partner is a sculptor caressing your form in admiration. You are not allowed to move during this game.

117

LUSTFUL GAME

You are a prostitute receiving a client. Inquire after his or her fantasies and special wishes, and be sure to ask for a very detailed description.

118

"Playing doctor" is still effective because it is not only a game with physical contact, but also involves authority and submission. When it is your turn to be the patient, let yourself be examined thoroughly!

SEXY PHOTOS

Pretend you are a photo model for an erotic magazine while your partner is the photographer giving you instructions about how to sit, stand, lie, move, etc. and encourages erotic poses.

119

120

VICTOR/VICTORIA

Try exchanging clothes with your partner. Then you can undress each other, and dress each other again, and undress each other...

121

SMALL TALK

Go to a party separately without arranging a meeting time beforehand. When you meet up, flirt with each other outrageously and let the surprise of the other guests at your behaviour animate you.

122

PARLEZ-VOUS ITALIANO?

Set aside a whole day for speaking a
foreign (or imaginary) language that your
partner doesn't understand. You'll be
forced to depend on your eyes and hands
for communication, and your predictable
daily routine will be absolutely altered.
You'll suddenly find yourselves dealing
with each other in new, creative ways.

123

The exciting experience of making love in an automobile–almost in public–becomes not only much more comfortable, but also more romantic, if you rent a Rolls Royce or an expensive sports car for a day–and begin the proceedings in proper style with strawberries and champagne...

124

Have you ever visited a drive-in movie theatre? Let yourself get carried away by the unique atmosphere, ideal for whispering secrets and necking.

125

Even when you are not embraced in a kiss, stretch out your tongue every once in a while during foreplay. It is not only an inviting sight for your partner, it also helps you keep your jaw and facial muscles relaxed.

126

A woman can reach new heights of ecstasy if she simultaneously or alternately contracts the vaginal and anal muscles during sexual intercourse. For men, too, vaginal contractions during penetration are an unbeatable sensation.

127

Women can experience various kinds of orgasm: the clitoral and the vaginal. But don't arrange these in a hierarchy. That only leads to tension and performance pressure! No kind of orgasm is better or worse than another—they are only different from each other.

128

The fabled female G-spot actually exists and is located in the vagina. Before you or your partner begin to feel for it with a finger, you should empty your bladder, since stimulating the G-spot also puts pressure on your urethra and can result in the desire to urinate. The easiest way to locate the G-spot is to crouch down and let your finger glide along the inner front side of the vagina. At the back of the pubic bone, you will feel a rough, wavy surface which differs from its surroundings. This is the G-spot. Through direct contact with fingers or penis, the circulation of blood to the G-spot increases, and it swells. It can take a while before the stimulation of the G-spot is experienced as sexually exciting, but it is definitely worth your while to allow yourself to slowly get familiar with the sensations it generates. The G-spot receives the greatest stimulation when a man enters a woman from behind.

The cervix is extremely sensitive, and deep penile thrusts can even be painful. However, you can experience the cervix as a source of pleasure if you run a finger around it smoothly.

129

130

A woman's pelvic floor muscle ("love muscle") determines the circulation within her genitalia and thus her degree of sensation during sex. It should therefore be exercised! While urinating, you can stop the flow by tensing the love muscle; relaxation resumes the flow. This exercise is particularly useful when becoming consciously aware of your love muscle.

131

TRAINING THE LOVE MUSCLE

Crouch down and guide your finger into the vagina. Then tense your pelvic floor muscle and feel the pressure on your finger. Then relax the muscle and tense it again.

Place a finger on your perineum while lying on your back. Then tense your love muscle until the tip of your finger has been drawn into your vagina and relax it again in short intervals.

132

Lovemaking on a waterbed is definitely worth a try. The wave-like movement of the surface is not only extremely comfortable, but also provides additional stimulation in response to your movements.

133

If you have a hard time communicating your sexual wishes to your partner, try writing them down at leisure, and invite your partner to do the same. Then exchange lists and sit down next to each other as you read them. This will easily lead to a conversation where you can speak openly. Perhaps you've even been having the same fantasy...

134

Try changing your position during penetration, for example, with a chair or a table.

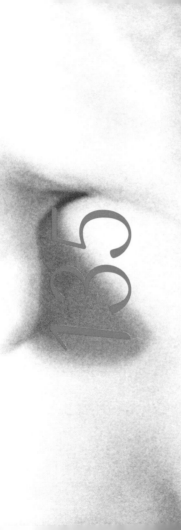

135

Stimulation of the anus with a finger while making love can be a very erogenous supplement for her and for him.

136

In positions where your hands are free, hold your partner's buttocks and exert pressure, alternating between a firm and a soft touch, for additional stimulation.

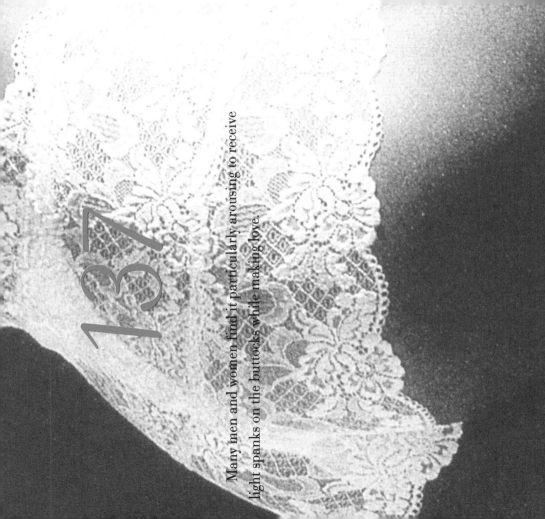

137

Many men and women find it particularly arousing to receive light spanks on the buttocks while making love.

138

TICKLISH SITUATIONS

Everywhere that your partner is ticklish is also a spot where he or she is highly sensitive. It is worth locating these areas for a particularly intensive and pleasurable erogenous massage. Be sure to check out foot soles and armpits, navel and hollows of the knees.

139

Women who experience penetration as uncomfortable due to a lack of moisture in the vagina should make sure they use a lubricant.

If you use condoms as a form of birth control or protection against sexually transmitted diseases, a lubricated condom may be a good solution.

140

Small injuries can easily occur during anal sex, so it is a good idea to always use a lubricant and be careful.

141

THE SWEETEST TEMPTATION...

Chocolate is one of the sweetest aphrodisiacs, particularly in combination with body painting. Try spreading your partner's body with chocolate syrup and then licking off every last trace.

142

NO SEX PLEASE!

Deliberately avoid having sex for a few days, and then make an "appointment" with your partner for the next time you make love. Anticipation can be the best foreplay!

143

Telling each other dirty jokes not only gets you into the right mood, but also loosens the atmosphere. Sex should not be a serious obligation! Do you know these two?

French Kiss

The princess went down to the pond and asked the frog, "Do I really have to kiss you before you can turn into a prince?" "No," the frog replied; "that was my brother. For me it's a blow job."

Two condoms ran into each other: "Man, you really look pale today!" "Yeah, well, yesterday I really got loaded."

GOOD MORNING

144

The best time for him to have sex is at 9 a.m., when his testosterone level is highest. Check it out for yourself!

145

9 a.m. works for her as well—it's a good start to the day, since a woman's testosterone level often adjusts to that of her partner over time.

146

COLOURS

According to a study, the three most erotic colours for her and for him are red-orange, dark blue, and violet. Surround yourselves with these colours during sex and see what happens.

147

The least erotic colour is gray—just think of a married couple trying to choose between couch upholstery of either mouse gray, ash gray or stone gray, and you can imagine that. So don't expect too much of sex if you are surrounded by gray.

148

Why not groom your pubic hair? Be inventive and take advantage of all the possibilities offered by cosmetics and hair care products to make yourself a sexy hairstyle.

149

Shaving your pubic hair can also look very sexy. Just beware: It is not particularly healthy for the skin on a long term basis and should remain the exception, rather than the rule.

150

Imagine you are a vampire, and quench your thirst with kisses and light bites of your partner's neck and throat.

Essential oils are not only stimulating in bath water—try letting a few drops of a stimulating scent that you both like fall onto your hair.

151

152

Healthy eating habits increase your general feeling of well-being and is therefore a prerequisite for good sex. Vitamins and minerals strengthen the nervous system, which can bring about an increase in your libido and the intensity of your orgasms.

153

If you lie on your back in such a way that your head is hanging down over the edge of the bed, you will probably experience a more intense orgasm, since more blood flows into your brain and your breathing is stimulated.

154

In the third week of a woman's menstrual cycle, (the days following ovulation) her testosterone level is at its peak and she experiences more desire than at other times of the month. Most women also reach a climax more easily during this period.

155

Playing a sport is not only healthy but also contributes to a fulfilled love life. Jogging, swimming, tennis, gymnastics or yoga, even simple stretching exercises boost your energy level, release tensions and increase your self-control and flexibility.

156

Treat yourself and your partner to a tongue-bath: Start with a French kiss and then work from the face over your partner's whole body until every bit has been completely covered by your tongue.

PHASES OF THE MOON

157

Keep an eye on the lunar phases—approximately one-third of all women are more sexually active during a full moon than at other times. Observe the moon and find out if this is true for you or your partner.

158

One good introduction to the full enjoyment of pleasure is a game aimed at developing the sense of touch: Your partner places various objects in a bag, and you guess what they are by feeling them. After a while, your hands will become so sensitised that you'll not only experience your partner's stroking much more intensively and pleasurably, but will also discover entirely new dimensions to the sense of touch.

159

THE EYES HAVE IT

The eyes are among the most sensitive areas of the body. As a result, attention to the eyes requires a special feel. Kiss your partner tenderly on the eyelids, and trace the eyebrows delicately with your tongue. Be sure to allow yourself plenty of time, since this form of physical contact can be extremely delicate and intimate.

160

Being overweight is not only damaging to your health, it also results in a lowering of testosterone levels.

In addition, high levels of cholesterol in your blood caused by a diet heavy in fat can lead to arteriosclorosis, which inhibits blood circulation in the body, including the genitals.

161

DREAM SEX

Go to bed early one night with your partner and set the alarm so that you are awakened from your dreams a few hours later. In this situation, sex can be particularly intense.

162

INSIDE OUT

Try using a condom with nibs inside out. He will soon discover that the nibs are not only pleasurable for her!

163

Take the testicles of your partner in your mouth and massage them with your tongue to create intense pleasure. Just be careful with your teeth, as testicles are very sensitive.

164

Don't neglect French kissing during foreplay. This is the one of the most intense joint experiences of lovemaking, which is probably why most call girls don't include kissing in their services. Make a date with your partner for a hot tongue-to-tongue rendezvous.

165

Kissing not only overcomes your experience of yourself as an individual to create a wonderful feeling of togetherness, but is also essential to building and maintaining trust.

166

Kissing during a climax is one of the most passionate experiences possible and will remain imprinted in your memory.

167

Women should tilt their heads back as far as possible during oral sex so as to be able to take as much of their partner's penis into the mouth as possible.

168

ADRENALINE KICK

When was the last time you rode on a roller coaster? Such experiences increase your adrenaline and release endorphines, the body's natural "drugs," which results in an increase in sexual desire.

169

NO SMOKING!

Nicotine is not only a neurotoxin, but also reduces the testosterone level. You will have a more fulfilled love life without cigarettes.

170

Direct stimulation of the highly sensitive clitoris is often uncomfortable for a woman who is already very aroused. Try stimulating the inside of the labia or the shaft of the clitoris, instead.

October is an excellent month to go on a romantic holiday with your partner—in this month the male testosterone level has its annual peak!

171

172

If you don't want to have children, at least not right now, make absolutely certain you use contraceptives if you want to enjoy sex. Nothing can inhibit free and relaxed lovemaking more than the constant fear of a pregnancy in the back of your head.

173

A GIFT FOR YOU

Wrap your genitals in gift wrap and make an agreement with your partner that the presents are not allowed to be unwrapped until after half an hour of foreplay. Then feel the tension mount until you can finally tear the paper apart...

174

Step into the shower with your partner and hold each other for ten minutes, letting your breathing coincide with your partner's and the sound of the water. Then turn off the water and stroke each other dry.

175

Showering together can be particularly stimulating when using a massage shower head. Change the water pressure setting frequently while petting each other.

176

Stimulate each other in the shower with the jet of water from a massage shower head. Start with the legs and continue upward, leaving the genitals to the end.

177

While enjoying that massage shower head together, decide on a length of time that you and your partner are not allowed to touch each other with your hands, and instead stimulate each other's genitalia with the stream of water. Keep the time fairly short, or you may not be able to stand such intense arousal!

178

The hollows of the knees are particularly erogenous skin zones. Enjoy an elaborate finger massage followed by stroking with the tongue on the back of your knees.

179

A man's penis is utmost sensitive directly after ejaculation. It is best to wait a few minutes before stimulating your partner again, and then begin by pleasuring the tip of the penis with your tongue.

180

Don't make technique your highest priority during sex. A fulfilled love life doesn't dependant on mastering a particular catalog of techniques, but on the degree to which you can express your emotions.

181

LET YOURSELF GO!

Problems letting go and achieving truly intense sex is often related to a fear of losing control. Allow yourself to switch off your mind and let yourself act according to your feelings! The more you lose control, the more intense the sex.

182

Lie down on your back next to your partner and concentrate on your breathing. Try to breath in time with your partner by breathing in and out at the same time. Relax like this for a few minutes until you can sense the field of energy that encloses you both.

183

Try staying still in embrace for at least ten minutes after penetration. When the man's erection fades, begin again with slow, smooth movements. You will be amazed how intense your desire becomes.

184

TOO SMALL, TOO SHORT?

Make an effort to free yourself of all preconceptions about sex. There is nothing that is right or wrong, only things that are fun or not fun: Only with this attitude can you really enjoy sex. Complexes kill sexual desire.

If you are busy worrying that your belly is too fat, your breasts are too small or your penis is too short, you can't be fully present and enjoy sex. Talk to your partner about your hangups (when you are not making love) to build up enough trust to let go of those issues.

185

INHIBITIONS?

One way to rid yourselves of inhibitions is to create a cozy atmosphere with dimmed light, undress each other slowly, and run your hands all over each others' bodies. Another exercise is to try crawling around the room on all fours with your partner. Talk to each other while doing this and maintain eye contact.

186

Spoil your partner sometime by concentratedly stroking and kissing your partner's face. Begin with the fingertips of both hands, than switch to the palms of your hands, and eventually use your mouth, lips and tongue. These tender moves are not only highly pleasurable, they also deepen trust between you.

187

Stand facing your partner and use your palms to stroke each other between the armpits and hips with up and down movements on both sides for several minutes. Switch to circular movements on both sides for several minutes, and then revert to the palms of your hands until you feel your desire rising.

188

Feet are another nice place to nibble. Try an erotic partner massage with the mouth—run your tongue over the sole of the foot, massage each toe individually with the lips, and don't forget the sensitive spaces in between the toes. Can you feel your whole body getting warmer?

189

Stroke your partner over the back, stomach and buttocks in swimming movements. To do this, move the palms of your hands in opposite directions if you were swimming the breast stroke. By varying the tempo of the movement, you create desirable counter currents.

190

Long fingernails are not so suitable for stroking with the fingertips as they easily scratch. If you have long nails, use the palms of your hands or your outstretched fingers instead.

191

Anal or vaginal penetration with a finger should definitely be avoided with long fingernails, since they could easily cause painful injuries.

192

Owing to the position of the thumb, the human hand is a natural "tool." Make use of the ideal possibilities that the thumb offers to rub your partner's skin gently between the thumb and fingers while stroking his or her erogenous zones.

193

Swinging is not only a great experience for children—a modified version of swinging can be part of foreplay. Your partner lies face down, and you sit down next to your partner, level with his or her buttocks. Grasp your partner by the hip and lift up slightly, then release. Repeating this motion first on one side, then on the other, creates a swinging movement which is both comfortable and stimulating.

194

A particularly exciting kind of kiss meanders from one ear to the other, by way of the mouth. Start this kiss with your lips, turn it into a French kiss at your partner's mouth and let it evolve back into a lip kiss on your way to the other ear. Or just the opposite: Start with the tongue, move into a lip-on-lip kiss and then move on with your tongue. Let yourself be surprised by the effect on your partner!

A woman's breasts are glands, which are much more sensitive than muscle. Be careful not to exert too much pressure when massaging or stroking them.

195

196

Circle your partner's breasts in a swimming motion (in opposite directions), starting at the sternum, and then stroke them with the hollow of the hand in up and down movements without touching the nipples. Repeat this for several minutes before stroking the nipples with your fingertips. This massage magically intensifies the stimulation of the nipples.

197

A stomach massage can be very relaxing, but should always be done softly, since the stomach muscles are very sensitive and too much pressure on the stomach is uncomfortable. The best method is to stroke it with your flat hand.

198

For a completely different type of stimulation, glide over the erogenous zones of your partner with the knuckles of your fingers. Try changing the speed and the pressure while doing so.

199

Whisper declarations of love or erotic fantasies into your partner's ear in a low voice that can just barely be heard. This sensuous act is not only effective owing to the power of a quiet voice, but also due to the intimate touch of your lips and breath on the ear, which is very sensitive.

200

Are You Coming?

If you have difficulties reaching a climax, give up the idea that this is the sole aim of your sexual activities. Instead, focus your attention on the activities themselves, and enjoy them without aiming for an orgasm. Without the stress factor of "having to come," you are likely to have an orgasm much more easily.

201

Why not try out the pleasures of a breast-to-breast massage? For this he needs to lie on his back while she sits on him and provocatively glides her breasts over his nipples.

202

Stand opposite each other, naked, and place your hands on your partner's shoulders. Look at each other from top to bottom and imagine that small fires are smouldering in your partner's skin that grow larger and larger and spread to you as well, until you feel yourself growing really hot and are literally "on fire" with desire.

203

Repeated contraction and relaxation of your anal muscle can be very erogenous. It will give you a warm feeling that spreads all the way to your head.

204
MUSCLE POWER

For women, the combination of anal muscle and love muscle (pelvic floor muscle) contractions can lead to intense excitement. Practice alternate and combined contractions and enjoy the sensations!

205

According to Taoism, the contraction of the anal muscle simultaneously massages the male prostate gland, which is stimulated to release more hormones.

Place your flat hand over the genitals of your (female) partner and exert gentle pressure while moving her from one side to the other. This stimulation not only excites her, but also arouses a feeling of warmth and security.

206

207

Taoism: The Nine Stages of Pleasure

According to Taoism, a woman's orgasm includes nine stages, each of which involves other parts of her body. This theory reflects early Taoist beliefs that the pleasure of both partners is essential to a fulfilled sex life, and allows the woman and (most importantly) her partner to identify the stage of satisfaction she is in.

Stage 1

The woman's orgasm begins on this level with deep breaths followed by sighs and the production of saliva in the mouth. This stage corresponds to stimulation of the lungs.

208

209

Stage 2

She kisses him while she stretches out her tongue. This stage corresponds to stimulation of the heart.

Stage 3

In this level she holds him tightly; her muscles are stimulated. The activation of spleen, stomach, and pancreas are included in this stage.

211

Stage 4

At this stage there is a flow of vaginal fluid that corresponds to stimulation of the kidneys and the bladder.

Stage 5

She starts to bite him, while her joints become soft.

Stage 5 is said to correspond to the stimulation of the bones.

213

Stage 6

She embraces him with her arms and legs and winds herself around him. This corresponds to the stimulation of the liver and the nerves.

Stage 7

In her excitement, she tries to touch her partner all over the body, which is associated with her blood beginning to boil.

215

Stage 8

She bites harder and gropes for his nipples, at the same time relaxing all her muscles, which correspond to this stage.

216

Stage 9

She gives herself to her partner completely and surrenders to a *petit mort* ("little death"). The entire body is involved in this stage.

Never stop flirting with your partner, even after you have been together a long time. Flirting is not only fun as you're getting to know each other, but is also essential to keeping a long-term relationship fresh.

217

218

PRELUDE TO A HOT NIGHT—
SUCCESSFUL FLIRTING

Successful flirting requires a healthy sense of self-confidence. You can only convey your interest playfully when you accept yourself just as you are and assume that someone else has every reason to take interest in you.

219

Flirting should be fun—an exciting game that includes a good dose of humour. Postpone more serious themes for another occasion in order not to spoil the playful mood.

220

Tell your partner about all the important details of your life to help her or him form a full picture of you and thus build up a sense of trust.

Of course you can't have the identical opinion as your partner on all issues, but it is crucial to respect your partner's opinion. This will also help create a harmonious atmosphere.

221

Clothes make the (wo)man! Don't dress too drab and conservatively when going out to flirt. It's better to be a bit too noticeable than not noticeable enough.
Pick an erogenous zone to display: the neck, your cleavage, your legs.

222

HERE'S LOOKING AT YOU, KID:

Eye contact is an essential element of flirting. Hold your glance steady and look deeply into the eyes of another. Passing glances give the wrong signal.

223

Your pupils automatically enlarge when you find someone attractive—and vice versa! So look for the small signals; it can really pay off.

Erotic literature can provide an exciting lead-in to foreplay. Of course the text has got to be something that you both like. Take turns reading anything from Sappho's love poems to J.G. Ballard's *CRASH*– all the while touching each other's bodies lightly . It won't be long before the fiction recedes into the background, and you start writing your own story!

225

A penetrating look over the frames of your glasses can also be extremely seductive. Try it—and if you don't wear glasses, put on a pair of sunglasses.

Take a newspaper with you into a café. Hold the paper in front of your face and throw a few unmistakable glances over the edge of the paper at the Object of your Desire. Repeat the "exercise" a few times, and you will soon find out what kind of effect your signals have.

226

227

Compliments play a great roll in verbal flirtation. But don't overdo it.
Begin with a bit of sincere flattery wrapped in a witty phrase.

228

Touch Me!

Fleeting touches intensify the flirt instantaneously. Try laying your hand casually on the hand or arm of the other person. Such touches become even more arousing when they appear to be coincidental and unintentional.

229

One very entertaining form of flirting is winking. It establishes a secret connection between you and the Object of your Desire, and lets your adventurous spirit be recognised. Try it out—the results are sure to be surprising.

230

When flirting, place your
glass on the table so that you
"accidentally" brush the arm or
shoulder of the person you are
flirting with each time you reach
for it.

231

When you stand up to go to the restroom in a cafe or bar, pass your partner as closely as possible, laying your hand almost casually on his or her shoulder.

232

Play with one of the objects on the table—a glass, a coaster, a pencil—and in the process, "unwittingly" stroke the other person's hand.

233

Use pauses in the conversation to smile at the other person—and allow the pauses to stretch out. A sustained and direct smile can easily lead to something more...

234

Making Contact

When glances have not succeeded in establishing contact (because your Object of Desire is not looking in the right direction...) stand up and lightly touch the person as you pass by. Then stop abruptly and excuse yourself with a deep gaze and an irresistible smile.

235

In order to flirt successfully, you must be able to accept compliments gracefully. Rejecting a compliment can very quickly destroy the atmosphere—and possible even insult the other person. If you push a compliment aside, you are indirectly telling the other person that she or he lacks good taste or even wants to make fun of you. Instead, thank the person graciously with a direct smile.

One good compliment deserves another—anything else would interrupt the flow of the flirtation. If a direct counter-compliment is not possible—for example, if someone compliments a woman on her hair, but is himself bald—then simply thank him for the nice compliment.

237

A STAR IS BORN

It is easy to become nervous in a charged situation like flirting. But becoming too tense gets in the way of spontaneous and witty repartée. In such situations, simply imagine yourself to be a great star giving an interview—but don't forget to focus on your interviewer, too.

238

The ability to listen is just as important as being a good conversationalist. Listening builds a level of trust that can be intensified through direct and sustained eye contact.

239

For women, the remark "I'm cold" remains a classic flirtatious comment. If the other person offers only his jacket instead of his arm for warmth, then he may be the wrong partner.

240

Helplessness has traditionally (and often disastrously) provided a classic opportunity for women to start a flirtation. As we know, women are anything but helpless. Happily, today this stereotype can be reversed—men can also use "helplessness" to garner the attention of the woman they are interested in by "accidentally" dropping a stack of papers or a bag of apples. The "right" woman will of course rush to help—and naturally start up a conversation.

241

DIRTY DANCING

Dancing makes it extremely easy to flirt with the entire body, and fast music can work just as well as blues. The right movements can demonstrate your intentions, call attention to yourself, lure the interest of the other person...

242

Try stroking the hair away from your face during a flirtation. It not only has a seductive effect, but also indicates a willingness to make contact when you "bare" your face.

243

SATURDAY NIGHT FEVER

Discos offer a good opportunity for flirtation, not only because of the dancing, but also because it is so loud that conversation can only take place when you stand very close to another person, or sit and speak directly into their ear. This inevitably brings you closer...

Don't try to flirt, either standing or sitting, with your arms folded in front of you! This posture signals distance and defensiveness.

244

245

A soft but deep voice intensifies a flirtation. Try it out—you'll see how it creates an intimate atmosphere.

246

INTUITION

Trust your intuition. Everyone has the ability to sense what is good for them and what is not. Intuition allows you to tell whether the Object of your Desire also finds you interesting. As soon as your intuition says that there's a tiny spark, you can take the initiative.

247

Order an exotic cocktail and react enthusiastically when you taste it. Then offer the glass to your partner to taste. This gesture is as discreet as it is effective.

248

In the course of a flirtation, talk about what you might undertake together. This will enable you to discover common interests and to convey that you are interested in more than a "one night stand."

249

IS THAT YOU?

To stike up a flirtation, address the Object of Your Desire questioningly with "Sarah?" or "Michael?" When the confused response comes that in fact he/she is someone else, apologise, smile, introduce yourself, and tell a short story about Sarah or Michael or whomever— and you're already involved in a conversation.

Buy two tickets for a concert, the movies or theatre. If you see an interesting person at the entrance, approach her or him and explain that your friend (a woman, if you're a woman; a man, if you're a man) had to cancel at the last minute, and offer the other person the "extra" ticket.

250

251

Spontaneously ask someone you are interested in meeting for advice. In a store you can inquire which jumper you should buy; in a restaurant, which wine suits your meal... Such little flatteries easily evolve into conversation because, let's face it, everyone is pleased when their advice is solicited.

252

KEEP YOUR EYES ON THE TRAFFIC

Have you ever flirted at a red light? It's not only fun and exciting, but with a little gesture indicating the next parking lot, can even lead to a date.

253

Start working on a crossword puzzle in a cafe. In a little while, without raising your head, absent-mindedly ask in the direction of the Object of your Desire for a word. Then suddenly sit upright, as if just awakened, and smile at the person—who by this time is doubtlessly intrigue.

254

»JE T'AIME«

Tone of voice is not only one of the most sensitive forms of expression, but can also have an especially stimulating effect and create intimacy. Literally try to "tune in" to your partner during foreplay by listening to romantic music (however you define it) and singing love songs.

255

A direct—if extremely bold—way to enter into conversation is to rush up and embrace someone spontaneously, and then a moment later apologise coquettishly with the words: "Please excuse me, but my ex boy/girl friend was standing there, and simply doesn't want to understand that it's all over." Now you have established not only a good theme for conversation but also body contact—the ideal prerequisites for an exciting flirtations.

256

Teasing someone shows you like him or her. A few flippant remarks, a witty response can create an extremely exciting tension in a conversation. But be careful not to go too far: Don't get sarcastic, or your effort may backfire.

257

If you notice that someone is shy, don't let your approach be too direct, or you might scare her or him away. Make hidden compliments and flirt with light hints until a sense of trust has developed.

258

You can tell if there is enough trust to build on in a flirtation if the other person can look you directly in the eyes without turning away, and if he or she can sustain a smiling gaze at you.

After a delicious initial flirtation, invite your partner to a café or bar. And don't destroy the mood by requesting separate checks! Going dutch is not romantic—at least not at this stage. And who knows? Perhaps the other person will suggest a date with a "Next time it's my turn"!

249

260

It's important to be punctual for a rendezvous. Don't keep the other person waiting in an attempt to "prove" your importance. It is more polite to appear on the scene too early than too late—tardiness can be insulting. Let your punctuality demonstrate your respect for your partner. It also goes without saying that you inform her or him in good time if you can't keep a date; don't keep silent out of a mistaken desire to avoid disappointing your partner. It is certainly worse to be stood up than to face making another appointment. If something beyond your control gets in the way of your rendezvous, let your partner know. In the age of cellular telephones you can call even from the middle of a traffic jam.

261

Don't end a date merely with a vague promise to get in touch soon; instead, set up another rendezvous right away. Nothing is more frustrating than eternal waiting. Furthermore, without a definite appointment, another problem arises—that of deciding whether it is too soon or too late to get in touch again.

262

SPIN THE BOTTLE

Make use of an old childhood game to bring yourselves closer to the point after a hot flirtation. You already know how it goes: Whichever of you two the bottle points to must remove a piece of clothing.

263

Foretelling the future is also a good method to move closer to one another after a successful flirtation. Invite your partner to hold out his or her palm for a reading. When you partner presents the requested palm, treat it to tender caresses—and "read" a glowing future!

264

LIP SERVICE

In a flirtation that has a certain end in mind, don't be too shy to make explicitly erotic references. Lick your lips every now and then to signalise your desire. A mouth rounded into "kissing position" sends a similar message.

265

Write your partner (once again) a love letter. Such romantic memories not only can serve as a great comfort in "bad times," but can also create new excitement in a long-term relationship.

266

Send your partner a gift certificate for 100 kisses—to be redeemed that same evening when he or she arrives home. You'll see what pleasure this romantic gesture creates, and what an effect such a greeting can have!

267

Make a night date with your partner in a park or other remote area—and don't forget to bring candles... and a blanket.

268

Take the time to return with your partner to the place where you first met. Refresh your memories of your shared past.

Hide little notes containing declarations of love, compliments, or your secret desires all over your apartment or house—or in the pockets of your partner's clothing. Games like this bring new swing into your love life.

269

270

LET'S GO TO MY PLACE!

Set up a rendezvous with your beloved in a locale close to your apartment—but first make certain that it is closed! The alternative lies right around the corner...

271

Invent a new love language just between you and your partner. There's almost nothing that provides a closer connection or more excitement that a language that only the two of you understand. Included in the vocabulary are nicknames known only to you and that you only use when you are together.

Give names to the various parts of your bodies, including the genitalia, that express what you feel when you stroke and kiss these parts. In this word game, you can create new designations for your actions, such as petting and kissing, and invent a new name for love-making itself. You can also provide new nomenclature for your sex toys—especially delicious here, of course, are words drawn from daily life!

272

Have you ever tried a "quickie" in an especially exciting place that carries the danger of discovery—for example, in the dressing room of a store, or an elevator between the third and tenth floors?

273

Classic and yet always exciting is a date in an auto—best in a parking lot at twilight or at a spot with a beautiful view at sundown. This is sure to get you into the right state of mind, and you'll feel as if you're doing it for the first time!

274

ILLEGAL PARKING

Role playing can bring new energy into a partnership. Try turning up in a policewoman's uniform and berating your partner for illegal parking. He'll certainly fall to his knees begging for mercy—and offer you an appropriate bribe. Will you accept...?

275

Is it time for a thorough cleaning of your apartment or house? Then order yourselves a day of maid service—you and your partner, wearing little more than a feather duster—and get to work. After all, love is better on a squeaky-clean floor...

276

Working together to create a meal for two can be a sensual prelude to a romantic night, especially if you both are naked as you cook and eat. What do you think the pudding will be?

277

Start a night of love with a mutual visit to a professional masseur. This is sure to put your bodies in the right mood.

278

Skinny-dipping allows every part of your body, and especially your genitals, to be softly caressed by the water. Make a date with your partner somewhere that nude bathing is permitted and allow yourselves to be swayed into the mood for love by the free feeling of a water massage without clothing.

279

People change—not only to adapt to different situations, but also with time. Always remember to ask what your partner's desires are, even if you have been together for a long time.

280

Always leave sufficient time for afterplay. A climax that ends in each person abruptly turning away from the other results in frustration, rather than enjoyment.

Hug your partner in your arms and tell them how much you enjoyed sex. Stroke your partner's whole body and allow the feeling of satisfaction to permeate the entire room. Allow the atmosphere recede slowly, for instance, by simply lying next to each other.

281

Pregnancy doesn't make sex suddenly into a taboo—in fact, there is almost nothing that is undoable throughout the entire pregnancy. In any case, talk to your doctor about it—she will be able to tell you whether there are any medical indications that require caution in your particular situation.

_282_

In the first phase of pregnancy the hormonal balance of mothers-to-be is rather topsy-turvy, and most women are truly not in the mood for sex. Loving and supportive partners should accept this and have a little patience—sometime around the end of the third month the situation often looks quite different.

283

The intimacy that connects partners during a pregnancy can intensify their shared sexual experiences. Incorporate your/her swelling belly into your love play, and see this time as an opportunity to experiment with new positions and means of loving each other.

284

Most people go about their everyday routine without thinking about it or taking time for the things we really want to do. Pay attention to your needs in every area of your life and make yourself aware of them. This will help you discover more about your sexual desires, as well.

285

Body language, or non-verbal communication, is the main means of communication during sex. With your body you can let your partner know what you don't like, what is good for you, how it could be better. Guide your partner's hand, direct your partner with your body—give your partner signals.

Say goodbye to ideals and idols and start loving yourself. You don't have to look like a bodybuilder or model to have a satisfied love life, just feel at home in your own body.

287

With all the various positions that are possible in sexual intercourse, there are four basic types from which all the others are derived: the man lying on the woman, the woman on the man, both lying next to each other, or the man entering the woman from behind.

Leopard in the Jungle

In this position, the woman kneels on the floor with her lower arms on the ground and her head resting on her arms. Her buttocks are raised up in the air. The man kneels behind her, massaging her hips and back, and she allows him to insert his penis deep inside her.

289

Bird in the Nest

The woman lies on her back and twines her legs around the hips of her partner, who kneels before her in a position to enter. This position allows both partners free hands and great freedom of movement.

290

Lotus Pair

Lotus pair is among the sitting positions. The man sits tailor-fashion, while the woman sits in his lap with her legs slung around his hips. A slow, swinging motion of their hips back and forth brings them together.

291

Give your partner the feeling that he or she is someone special. The more you strengthen this sense in him or her, the more trust will develop, along with a readiness to lose control. Something as simple as a bouquet of flowers presented for no reason at all can say volumes!

292

Tongue Teasing, Lip Love

Make it a point not to always kiss the same way–predictable kissing is boring after a while. And there are so many variations to be tried!

Touch each other with the tips of your tongues outside your mouths, alternating a darting, flicking motion and a circular, dancing motion.

Play with each other's tongues inside your mouths by rubbing the upper sides of your tongues together.

Complement a passionate tongue kiss with gentle sucking to make it all the more passionate.

With your lips and tongue, concentrate on your partner's upper lip sometime, and save the lower lip for another session.

Explore the inside of your partner's mouth with your tongue, from the upper palette to the lower jaw, and delight in the different sensations your tongue experiences in the process.

293

294

Open your eyes while kissing occasionally and maintain eye contact with your partner. Closed eyes don't necessarily increase your pleasure!

295

Try making loud kissing noises while kissing sometime! It's so much more encouraging and arousing than quiet kisses.

296

PILLOW TALK

Even more exciting are little compliments whispered between kisses, or while you kiss your partner with your lips.

MOUTH-TO-MOUTH

Try to share a sip of champagne while kissing. Champagne will never have tasted quite so prickly before!

297

298

Play a childhood game with spaghetti or strands of licorice. The partners take opposite ends into their mouths and work as quickly as possible to the middle, where the longing mouths, lips and tongue meet!

299

Pieces of candy, ice cubes, and chewing gum are well suited for games with the tongue. Especially erotic and challenging: See how often you can pass a raw egg yoke back and forth between your lips.

300

THE COURAGE TO MASTURBATE

People used to think that giving oneself pleasure had dangerous consequences for the body. We now know that that is not the case. Set aside any inhibitions and live out your fantasies!

301

Masturbation, like lovemaking, requires time. Do not overstimulate your clitoris or penis, but stroke it softly, with pauses, in order to make your imaginary love game last longer.

302

Masturbation doesn't have to be a lonely pursuit—you can watch your partner pleasuring her- or himself, or let your partner watch you. You can learn a great deal about your partner's likes and dislikes this way.

303

Use your fantasy while masturbating. Create new dream creatures and situations. If you open up the power of your imagination, you'll discover many new ideas for love games with your partner.

304

Turn to films and literature for inspiration. Call up individual scenes into your memory and relive them, or develop them further. Or place yourself in the role of Micky Rourke or Kim Basinger in *9 1/2 Weeks*.

305

To get into the right mood, dare to call a telephone-sex service.

306

Use your voice when you masturbate. The sounds of your own sighing, moaning or screaming can be extremely stimulating.

307

Giving yourself pleasure in an almost public spot is a particular kick. Do it in the locker room at the swimming pool, or in the sauna behind a curtain...

308

One of the reasons for masturbating is to become familiar with your own body and its desires and preferences. Set off on a lust-filled journey of self-exploration and discover your most erogenous zones.

309

You scratch my back, I'll scratch yours

A sense of warmth is highly pleasurable and relaxing. Stroke your partner with a warm, wet flannel and use your other hand to dry the skin off with a towel that has been warmed on the radiator.

310

Being handcuffed or tied to the bedposts is not everyone's cup of tea. It can be more exciting to agree with your partner that one of you will put your hands behind your head and will not allowed to move, while the other stimulates the genitals orally or manually. This is more exciting because the other person *could* move at any moment!

311

Wrap your partner in a curtain from the shoulders down so that the naked body can be seen through the fabric, and then stroke his or her whole body. You have probably never touched, or been touched, like this before! It is especially arousing to stimulate your partner's genitals whilst they are wrapped in the curtain, and to unwrap them only when they can't stand the tension any more and ask you to.

312

Use a soft eraser to caress the skin of your partner, frequently altering pressure and pace.

313

A "HOT" SHOWER

Did you know that the alternation of hot and cold showering can increase your sexual energy to a whole new level? The changing temperatures strengthen the adrenal glands and nerves leading to your sexual organs. Such stimulation makes the sexual organs stronger and provides for better circulation. Why not make this shower part of your daily routine?

ABSTINENCE MAKES ONE HORNY

Occasional fasting boosts your sexuality and improves the function of your glands and sexual organs. Just a few days are enough to pep up your libido. Be sure to drink more than usual while you fast, and to gradually build up to your normal diet when your period of fasting is over.

314

315

TEATIME

Various teas or infusions available at the supermarket or pharmacy can have an aphrodisiacal effect (read the package inserts!).

Aniseed strengthens cardiac function and speeds up hormone production. It is a good pleasure stimulant. Gentian tea activates the gonads, thus increasing desire. Saint John's Wort has well-known anti-depressant and mood-brightening properties, and also gives the nervous system a boost, particularly the genitals. An infusion made from white radish stimulates the muscles in the genital area. Tee made with the leaves and roots of cloves stimulate the corpii cavernosae in the penis that bring about erection, while peppermint tea prolongs erections and intensifies your sense of touch.

316

The essential oil derived from "false pepper" has a stimulating effect on the genital muscles. The full effects become apparent about half an hour after taking it. Place two drops on a sugar lump and allow it to dissolve slowly in your mouth.

317

For truly fulfilled sexuality, beginning from a state of complete relaxation and disengagement from your daily life is just as important as the stimulation and arousal of your senses and body that.

Taking a bath with one of the following combinations of essential oils is one fabulous method of achieving this. First fill the bath with water and only then add about 15 drops of the oil, so that it doesn't evaporate before you can enjoy it. It is best not to soak in an oil bath for longer than 10 minutes.

318

A bath with lavender or valerian oil is soothing and eases everyday stresses. If your nerves are on edge, a bath with melissa balm oil can have a calming effect.

Bathing with rosemary or horse-chestnut oil will improve your circulation a boost, which is also beneficial to your libido. Pine oil has an invigorating and refreshing effect. Hayseed is another essential oil that energises, and is particularly suitable for mature skin.

319

A sea-salt bath both detoxifies your body and stimulates your senses. Add about a pound of sea salt to a full tub, and restrict yourself to 15 minutes in the water.

A lemon bath has a calming effect, but also promotes circulation to the skin, thereby increasing its sensitivity to touch. Soak six sliced lemons in a bowl of water for several hours, then pour the water through a sieve. Add this to the bath water and bathe for up to 15 minutes.

Why not treat yourself and your partner to an entire Wellness Weekend? Gather your provisions and do the shopping on Friday so the fun can begin. Try a bath with some of the essential oils, or herbal teas. Devote your full attention to relaxed bodily pleasures. You will find that it has an effect on your libido, as well! A scented bath *à deux* can be a real turn-on: the addition of 3 drops jasmine oil, 4 drops ylang-ylang oil and 10 drops of sandalwood oil is sure to set your heart racing.

320

321

Buttermilk is an excellent alternative to soap for your face—your skin will become firmer and tiny wrinkles will even disappear.

322

Not only is the skin the largest organ of the body, it also plays a large role in sexuality since it is the only means we have of perceiving the sense of touch. Take the time to treat your skin well so that it maintains its sensitivity.

323

One of the most sensitive parts of skin is the face. Steam baths with chamomile or sage improve circulation and have a cleansing effect on oily skin. They should not be used on dry skin, however.

324

Face masks with natural ingredients are quick and easy to make at home, and are an important part of skin care:

Apple mask: Finely slice and cook an apple with half a cup of water until soft. When cool, puree it with a fork and add two teaspoons of honey. Apply the mixture to clean skin and leave it on for 20 minutes. Wash off with warm water. This mask will clarify and soften the skin.

Egg yolk mask: Whisk an egg yolk with a teaspoon of olive oil and a splash of lemon juice in a water bath (over, but not in, a pot of hot water), stirring constantly. When the mixture is homogenous, apply it to the cleansed skin. After 20 minutes, rinse with warm water.

This mask nourishes your skin. The cholesterol in the egg yolk will make your face soft and supple, and smooths cracked skin.

326

Egg white mask: For firmer skin with smaller pores, beat an egg white with a drop of lemon juice until it is foamy. Apply the mask onto clean skin, using a wide brush, let it dry for a short time, and then remove it with warm water.

327

Strawberry mask: Mash five strawberries with a fork and stir in a spoonful each of double cream and honey. Apply it to the cleansed skin, let it work for 20 minutes, and wash off with warm water. This mask has a soothing effect on the skin.

328

Cucumber mask: This is especially recommended for those with blemished skin. Simply cleanse your face and cover it with not-too-thin slices of cucumber. Place a damp tea towel over them for ten minutes, then remove.

Potato mask: Use a fork to mash a cooked potato and add two tablespoons of cold milk and three drops of lemon juice. Apply the mask to clean skin and let it rest for ten minutes. Use warm water to remove the mask. This is appropriate for oily skin, as it removes the shiny layer.

330

Quark (or *fromage frais*) mask: Combine two tablespoons of quark or another unripened cheese and one tablespoon of honey. Apply this to cleansed skin. Allow the mask to work for 20 minutes, then rinse well with warm water. This mask is especially designed for dry skin.

Elbows quickly become rough and unpleasant. To keep them soft and smooth, dip your elbows into two small bowls containing warm almond oil for a few minutes. Then brush the rough areas with a pumice stone and rinse under warm water. Following this treatment, rub your elbows with avocado peel or with an emollient body lotion.

332

Playing games relaxes the mind and energises the rest of you! How about a game of dice: For a one you get a kiss, if you roll a three you have to remove one article of clothing, and if you get lucky six, your partner has to fulfill a secret desire of yours...

333

A dildo is an artificial penis, a plaything many women enjoy using when giving themselves pleasure. But it can also be a fun addition to lovemaking—perhaps he can use it to get her really hot during foreplay before offering "the real thing." Dildos vary in size between 16 and 35 cm/6 and 14 inches.

334

A vibrator can be exciting not only for her but also for him. Draw the vibrating tip of the vibrator over her erogenous zones and then over his penis. This will set free a tremendous orgasmic energy.

335

Vibrators, electric massagers of various shapes and sizes, are chiefly used to simulate the clitoris. They provide for especially good masturbation by making possible several consecutive orgasms. But they are also good for sex with a partner. Remember, fantasy knows no bounds.

336

A cockring vibrator offers two sex toys in one. The penis ring allows the male partner to sustain himself considerably longer, while the egg-shaped vibrator stimulates the clitoris and brings a woman to orgasm.

337

GYMNASTICS, ANYONE?

A love swing allows a whole new erotic dimension to be explored. The female partner steps into two loops attached to the ceiling and hangs from them. Her partner approaches her either standing or kneeling and enters her. The swinging movement produces a marvellous pressure in the abdomen, resulting in an unimaginable orgasm.

338

Water, the source of life, also offers help with love. Take advantage of a heavy summer shower to make love on the balcony or in the garden. The prickling rain on your skin together with the distant heavens allow you to become one with Nature.

339

MYSTERIOUS GEISHA BALLS

Are you familiar with the so-called geisha balls, or love balls, used in Japan? The pair of hollow metal balls, each of which contains a smaller ball within itself, are gently introduced into the vagina. The slightest movement causes them to emit vibrations, creating an exciting erotic massage that can lead to orgasm.

340

Geisha balls are also delightful when making love as a pair. They serve as a wonderful means of increasing the stimulation at climax—but in this case, insert only one ball.

341

To sustain an erection, you can slide a cockring over the penis. This also has the advantage of stimulating the woman's clitoris. Cockrings are made of various materials: steel, brass, leather, and in the Orient, even of ivory.

342

VARIETIES OF ICE

Ice can have not only a prickling effect—it also tastes good. Take a fruit-flavoured or ice-cream ice cube and rub it over your partner's erogenous zones for a double treat.

343

TONIGHT'S SPECIAL....

Take a journey of discovery by concentrating fully on one zone of your partner's body. You can take your time with her breasts, for example, gently exploring them in minute detail, to the last pore of her skin. Don't limit yourself to using your hands, but be creative and get to know the chosen area with every part of your own body.

344

CAPTIVATING GAMES

There are more than a few people for whom pain is stimulating. Have you ever had such fantasies? Perhaps of being tied to the bed or to a chair while your partner has total power to do anything she or he wants with you?

345

Search out objects that you could use to make your partner squirm, even suffer. Be creative! You don't actually have to *use* every item in your collection—even the threat of doing so can be exciting!

346

Exchange roles to discover which one offers you more pleasure—the active or the passive position. In playing such games, only go as far as both partners are willing, and don't do anything solely in order to please your partner.

347

Tattooing has become popular again. Many people have tattoos on their arms, shoulders, legs, ankles or neck. Tattoos in places that only your partner sees, of course, hold a special charm. If you want a tattoo, choose the studio carefully. Seek advice and pay particular attention to the level of hygiene.

348

Piercing is also extremely fashionable. Everywhere you look there are pierced eyebrows, noses, navels. There are of course also more erotic variations, such as lip or tongue rings, which serve as toys in kissing.

Here, too, it is important to find a piercing studio that offers competent advice and a high standard of hygiene.

349

Piercing can also be carried out in the intimate body areas, for example through the nipples or labia. These forms of piercing are guaranteed to bring a new element of pleasure into your lovemaking, but they require full awareness of possible health risks. Of course there are also more "harmless" pieces of intimate jewelry: labial clips, penis rings and chains.

350

The imagination knows no boundaries in the use of lubricants. Of course, they are chiefly used for anal sex or with dildos, but try rubbing your whole body with the medium. It will be a totally new experience!

Only water-based lubricants should be used. They are easier on the skin and interfere less with latex condoms, gloves, or finger caps. Fat-based lubricants such as Vaseline also reduce sensitivity.

351

SEXY MENU

How would it be to turn your partner on with a meal? Serve it naked, in seductive underwear, wearing only an apron, or with one piece of clothing less per course...

352

THE WETTER, THE BETTER

Lubricants are not only useful when they are really needed, as with anal sex or when a woman would like to be wetter, but also are an excellent aid for massage or masturbation.

353

TUB SEX

A bathtub helps not only with relaxation and the creation of the right mood. Stay in the tub! But be careful to choose positions that don't run the danger of allowing you to fall over, slip, or bruise yourself on the fixtures. Otherwise bathtub fun will land you in serious hot water!

354

Bathing in a whirlpool is especially exciting. If you haven't got one at home, you can begin a night of love by visiting a whirlpool at a swimming pool or sauna. Let yourself fall into the mood, and enjoy the anticipation of everything that the night has in store.

355

A shower can be used to create steam heat that does more than open your pores. Transform your bathroom: exchange the cold electric light for candles, cast a spell according to your imagination by means of scented candles or incense sticks, and make love in a light summer shower with an exotic jungle rain—just be careful not to slip.

356

Take your partner out on his or her birthday to something completely unexpected: a striptease joint, a table-dance bar, a peep show. Stimulate your appetite for the main gift waiting at home...

357

FINGER FOOD

Bring a complete meal of aphrodisiac finger food along to bed and have a picnic. Dunk mushrooms, asparagus, artichoke leaves, okra, and celery stalks into dips made with avocado, garlic, appropriate herbs and "hot" spices. The dips are fun to lick not only from the vegetables.

358

Sex with three or four participants can be a great temptation and a great challenge, and take your love life in completely new directions. However, you must be absolutely certain that your wishes coincide with your partner's concerning the number and sex of the other partners, and is not just going along for your sake—otherwise your own pleasure will also be spoiled.

359

If you want to have group sex with three or four partners, begin by eliminating the danger of jealousy by establishing a sound basis of trust with your own partner, and also with the other participants.

And practice safe sex.

360

Swinger clubs offer a good opportunity to try out group sex. These are meeting places for pairs with similar ideas of exchanging partners. But don't worry—there are no wild orgies here! The pairs first get acquainted in a comfortable atmosphere before gradually getting down to business. The clubs offer all kinds of "ingredients" that are perhaps not always available at home. One is free to try out many different things according to the motto, "Everything is possible; nothing is necessary."

361

For the sex-hungry, the internet has a lot to offer. In addition to information on all aspects concerning sex, mail-order houses for sex toys and more, there are also erotic chat rooms in which one can talk with like-minded people. An enormous variety of chat rooms offer something for everyone, from flirting or dating to live sex with a web camera. But be careful: Many rooms are rather expensive, in more ways than one.

362

Body painting makes love more interesting. To experience a whole new kind of stimulation through pictures, discover your own body and that of your partner as a work of art and express your emotions and sense of fun in colours. On this subject, take a look at Peter Greenaway's film *Pillow Book*—but turn down the sound. The best dialogue is written on Ewan McGregor's flesh.

363

Never put yourself or your partner under pressure when it comes to sex, because anxiety can all too easily turn lust and desire into frustration!

364

To make sure sex doesn't become simply routine, create space and time for yourself and your partner. Treat yourself to love weekends and holidays entirely devoted to yourselves as a couple, your love, and your lust.

Trust and respect are necessary to ensure that that "good sex" remains a part of long-term relationships. Respect the word "No," develop the trust it takes to talk openly about everything, be open to new ideas, and NEVER let sex become routine. Remember that even after many years, your partner wants to be courted, seduced, and overcome as much as the first time. If you remember one tip from this book, let this be it.

365